Encouraged as a teenager to pursue writing, she attended university to study theatre and performance, combining her main interests: drama, and writing. Diagnosed with depression, anxiety and PTSD at twenty-two, and after being in and out of therapy, she put pen to paper to deal with her diagnosis. After the death of her dad in 2022, she wrote letters to him in the form of poems because he loved her writing and loved when she achieved things she wanted from life, even when life wasn't kind. Never published, she wanted to share her thoughts and feelings with people that have experienced love, loss, and a mental health diagnosis.

Rigby, Maskell and Price. A family that has loved and lost but always have each other. Thank you for everything you gave me.

Special mention for Gareth Utting who inspired so many to write and keep on writing.

Elle Ritchie

LOVE, LIFE, DEATH AND THERAPY

AUSTIN MACAULEY PUBLISHERS™

LONDON • CAMBRIDGE • NEW YORK • SHARJAH

A CIP catalogue record for this title is available from the British Library.

ISBN 9781035833184 (Paperback)
ISBN 9781528974585 (ePub e-book)

www.austinmacauley.com

First Published 2023
Austin Macauley Publishers Ltd®
1 Canada Square
Canary Wharf
London
E14 5AA

For the people at Austin Macauley Publishers who not only read my work but liked my work and wanted to give it a chance and a cover.

One Last Call

Hey, Dad, it's me,
I'm calling from Cornwall, and I just wanted to say,

I don't know the time and I can't remember the days,
Ever since you left us, each day feels strange.
But I wanted to call you anyway.

To see how you are,
To see how you've been,
All I want is to talk with you again.

If I had known that Monday the words that we spoke would
have been our last,
I would have let go everything from the past.

All that anger, hurt and pain,
I would let all that go just to speak words I thought I would
never say,
If all that meant was being able to see you and talk with you
for one more day.

First Christmas Without You

This will be our first Christmas with you gone,
This winter and last year has been a lonely one.

We have never had a Christmas without you,
I knew this day was coming, but I didn't want it to.

I cannot stand the thought that you are no longer here,
A future without you in it is becoming unclear.

This was never supposed to happen.
But we live and die at random.

But for one last time,
For one last day,
Have Christmas with us.
I wish that you could stay.

Anxiety

In my mind all the thoughts are a jumble
I open my mouth, but I start to mumble,
No sound,
No voice,
I begin to stumble.

I try to walk but my legs won't move,
I'm frozen to the spot,
I don't know what to do.

This feels like forever.
This feels like an age,
All I'm doing is fighting between fear and rage,
I'm trapped in my own mind that has become a cage.

All these thoughts are setting me on edge,
All these thoughts telling me I'm better off dead.

But that's the truth about our society,
We're all out here coping with depression and anxiety.

Toddler in Your Brain

Having anxiety is like having a toddler in your brain,
You're running around after them telling them to put a coat
on because it might rain.

But they do not want to go outside today,
They do not want to go out to play.
They do not want to go outside,
They'd rather stay indoors while you seek, and they hide.

You've said it'll be alright when they get there,
But they're sat on the staircase with a scowl and one sock on
and really don't care.

You plead, you beg, you even bribe,
After all this exhaustion you're contemplating staying
inside.
The toddler can be very convincing,
But remember that you're in charge and trying to do the
right thing.

Scoop up the toddler and get them dressed,

Because at the end of the day, you're in control and do know best.

You eventually get out and the toddler has calmed down,

You can overcome anxiety, get up, go out and have a good time.

Head Space

There isn't a carpet in my room anymore,
Instead, the clothes from the drawers cover the floor,
There're crumbs in the bed sheets, that's happened before!
I can see pasta stains on my T-shirt, which is getting harder
to ignore.
I should probably go back to therapy!
But the past is a place that I left behind closed doors.

In Her Genes

I wonder what it's like to be in her genes
How simply she fits between the seams.
She is not dictated by the confinement of her DNA.
She does not sit and think and wander each day,
What time to take her medication and in what way.
Three tablets at night with water
Two with food in the morning,
Being sure to read the side effects and warnings.
She sits there, comfortably fitting,
In the genes that she was given.

Depression

Flirting with death,
Teasing the time,
Living in a world that doesn't feel like mine.

It all ends eventually,
Maybe tomorrow,
Maybe today,
We can never really tell, we can never really say.

I wonder when my time will come.
Where will it end and how is it done?
Maybe asleep.
Maybe awake.
Whatever happens, that is my fate.

I don't belong in this world that I don't have room to move
in,
I often wonder how long I have left,
Unless I choose it.

Grief

I had been grieving,
Grieving for years.
My mother said, 'Stay strong now and dry those tears.'

But the grieving became heavy, it felt like a burden.
Loud voices, inside a dark cloud and no one else could hear
them.

But I could hear their cries,
I could feel their pain.
And once I let them inside my head, my life would never be
the same again.

I grieve for so much,
 Because so much is lost.
The fragility of life,
There is a price and there is a cost.

I really did think that the worst was over,
I thought I no longer had to look over my shoulder.

I had already lost a baby and thought nothing in this life
could be worse.

But I was wrong,

Once again Grief was at my door just like a curse.

My father died.

He passed away in June,

So, there was grief by my side once more whispering,

'I am here for you.'

Strangers, Like My Family

A family dinner isn't as it used to,
When you don't really know the person sat opposite you.
They have familiar names and familiar faces,
But not being there when it mattered has its implications.

Strangers, like my family,
They never really knew me.
They had their titles and their names,
But to call them family now isn't the same.
They were always around throughout my life,
Back when the word 'family' used to apply.
But now as I'm getting older,
I realise that they are not who I thought they were.

Boys Will Be Boys

I was never taught to fear those close,
But strangers instead,
'Let a boy walk you home at night.' That's what they said.

But that boy,
That person I knew,
He was the one that caused damage he could never undo.

A lifetime of trauma,
A lifetime of pain,

After that night,
I never let a boy walk me home again.

Numb

Every day is a blur,
Every day I do not see,
What I have right in front of me.

I'm not really here,
I can't seem to feel,
What once was there,
Is no longer real.

My Own Company

I'm content with my own company,
The world outside isn't as it seems.
I prefer to sit with my sadness and grief,
Because at least I know where it is.

Doom Scroll

Doom Scroll,
It's 4 am, I need to stop, but I won't be told.
I can't stop,
I won't stop,
This obsession,
This addiction,
It has me glued to my phone.

You Will Hear Me

A world of poems.
A world of words.
This is how I will be heard.

No one hears me if I speak,
Even if I raise my voice, shout or scream,
I know that they won't believe me.

'But there were no signs!'
That's what they'll say,
Even though I took medication every day.

Every morning I'd wake up warily,
Knowing someday I would be back in therapy.

'But there were no signs!'
'We didn't know!'
I hear, even though the scars on my arms were on show.

'She seemed normal!'
'She seemed fine!'
'How are we only finding out about this after she died?'

So, I'll write and write and write some more.
And people will know about my life from before,
Before all this happened.
Before all this time.
They can read all about a life,
That used to be mine.

Crossroads

Crossroads,

Find me at the Crossroads.

I'm here looking for the path that I was once shown.

But now that I'm here, I don't know which way to go.

I'm Alice in Wonderland, I've fallen down the rabbit hole.

Thoughts

The TV is on,
But I can't hear any sound,
I'm trying to focus,
But these thoughts that are too loud.

Life Gone Wrong

There's part of the bed that I don't sleep on,
There's a part of me that thinks I was raised wrong.
There's a life that I thought I wanted for so long,
But as the years go by, the dream of that life has gone.
Somehow,
Somewhere,
Life went wrong.

We're All Ghosts

Waiting for death is exhausting,
We call it living and ignore it.
We become ghosts who are forever haunting.
Roaming the earth, distorted.
But we never rest,
Even in death,
For as long as there are those still in mourning.

Hello, Stranger

Hello, stranger.
Who are you?
Do you recognise me too?
I feel like I did,
I feel like I should.
But when I try to remember, it's just no good.

I was like you once, I think.
With the cigarette smoke and holding a drink.

You were like me once,
You used to be kind,
Now when I think of you, I lose my mind.

Who are you?
Where did you go?
Did you try and find me, so you could finally know?
Know who you are.
Know who you were.
There're so many versions they're now a blur.

But I'm here, I'm real,
And you are too,
I really hope one day you can find yourself,
So, you can finally speak your truth.

"All the World's a Stage"

This is just a play,
This is all make believe,
I don't always understand the life I lead.

Help me escape,
Help me runaway,
Help me find myself again.

All the world's a stage,
And this is mine,
But it's a world that I want to leave behind.

Don't let tomorrow come,
Allow this moment to be mine,
Exploring a world that I have found.

I know my lines,
I know what I have to say,
Because the play is the same every day.
The same story with different players,
In a world in which I am the creator.

Help me escape this world that I have made,
Help me escape this part that I wish I never played.

You Know Who You Are

Why did this happen?
What have you done?
You've turned me into someone I didn't want to become.

You made me believe that this was something more,
When it was just you and me behind that door.

I felt things I knew I shouldn't have,
And I knew that you did too,
All I wanted was for you to tell me the truth.

You knew what you were doing,
You knew I wouldn't speak,
My feelings for you made me weak.

But you abused my trust,
You abused your career,
Me saying something was your greatest fear.

Nothing happened between us, not really.
But I wasn't imagining things,
You told me you had feelings.

You know who you are,

You know what you did,

And now you're at home with your wife and kids.

So, you never again have to think,

Behind that door, unseen,

With that girl in that room

And something that should never have been.

Writing Is Therapy

If I focus on writing, I don't have to think about anything else.
I can keep writing until the problems in my head start to make sense.

If I set goals for myself, I know I am moving forward,
Since I have started writing,
I have found out what is important.

Chosen Career

I often think about my friends and their chosen careers,
Social worker,
Teacher,
The military,
Paths carefully architected for years.

Everyone appears to have somewhere they belong, but not me.
I've never known what I wanted to be.

I have never had a career drive,
I've always done what I can to get by,
I like what I like and try to thrive.

There're gaps in my C.V.
There are gaps in my memory.
I can't remember who I am,
Or how I want to be seen.

Long Distance

Long distance relationships,
Long distance friendships,
Long distance family.
Long distance, it is the way it must be.

Everyone at arm's length,
So that nobody can get too close,
I hurt the ones that I love the most.

I am alone because I've made myself that way,
I am alone because I push people away.

New Love

I fell in love with an idea and a vision,
I became someone new each time that I was with him,
We don't stress, we just talk,
And when we're alone together, we move in perfect rhythm.

Movie Love

I like old movies,
'The Breakfast club,' 'Pretty Woman'
And 'Breakfast at Tiffany's.'

I like old romance,
Throw a lasso around the moon,
Or ask me to dance.

I'm a sucker for a remix,
Give me an 'Easy A.'
I'm all for John Hughes,
Give me Ferris Bueller any day.

What happens after he rescues her?
She rescues him right back.
I'll happily wait a lifetime,
For a boombox and John Cusack.

Heartbreak

Too many memories stolen away,
Too many times I should have left but instead stayed.

There have been enough tears because of you,
There have been too many times I've been untrue.

When will this stop?
Where does this end?

I want to be who I was without you, again.

Body Count

Initials of names,

I remember every single one.

What they drank and where they came from.

Why do I remember those who have forgotten all about me?

Not even my name,

Just another blurry face,

I suppose that is the way things are,

I guess that is the way it must be.

Not the One

Why do I get so sad because of you?
I knew exactly what you were going to do.
I never asked you for a lot.
But I was trying to put you in a box,
And make you out to be something you're not.

Unconditional Love

Don't tell me stories about Romeo and Juliet,
Tell me about Burton and Taylor instead.
Not a love worth dying for,
But love that means trying more.
I'm not asking for love to be easy,
All I'm asking is for someone to love me, unconditionally.

Enough is Enough

He held my hand,
He kissed my lips,
He spoke words that would later contradict.

We broke each other down,
And we tried to build ourselves back up,
But after so long, after so much trying,
I think enough is enough.

Without you

I spent so much time in your company,
I forgot all about the real me.

I didn't know who I was without you,
Everywhere you went, there I was, too.

But now I'm happy to spend time alone.
I am happier on my own.

Strangers Share a Bed

You lay on your side, and I'll lay on mine.
Remembering the life we have left behind.

Maybe one day we'll meet again, in the middle of the bed,
Maybe then we'll remember all the words we once said.
All those I love yous and all the laughter.
But now I'm not sure what happens after.

When the lights are turned out
And when you roll away,
I lay there wandering if we'll ever touch again.

Familiar bodies in a familiar room,
Was this a love burnt out too soon?

But we're both so quiet,
We're both so still,
I wanted a life with you,
To feel fulfilled.

It's now two in the morning,
I am awake, beside you here,
Waiting for the you I once knew to reappear.

What was once two people in love,
Has now disappeared.

Be Your Own Woman

Want some advice?
Never listen to a man.
Not your brother or father,
Speak up for yourself,
And make a stand.

Trust yourself above all others.
Never doubt your instincts for another.

Be your own woman,
Whatever that might mean,
Don't take advice from men,
Make sure that you are heard and seen.

Healing Trauma

I've been trying to unlearn so much shit,
Deconstructing my trauma, bit by bit,
I'm trying on some healing,
To see if it fits.

Sober

Since I've not been drinking,
I've started clearly thinking,
It's about time I started living,
There is so much life that I have been missing.

Perfect Life

A perfect life comprised of perfect moments,
Moments that aren't spent looking over your shoulder,
The days in bed,
The books that are read,
The things we appreciate as we get older.

Strong. Independent. Female

Une Solo.
Only one.
But not lonely,
I'm the one that takes care of me.
I'm Miss Independent,
Miss Strong Female Lead.
I'm Sandra Bullock in Miss Congeniality.
I can eat red meat and still be a graceful Queen Bee.
I'm Wednesday Addams,
I don't take shit from anybody.

You're Okay

When you spend so long trying to recover,
You realise you weren't prepared for what comes after,
So many years of hurt and pain,
So much time thinking you would never be the same again.

You realise you were right; you are not the same as before,
You have grown to be so much more,
Now you know who it is that you are.
You know that you have worked hard and come so far.

Stay in the moment.
Don't lose your mind,
You can get through this,
Remember, you are going to be fine.

Life Changes

When I was young, I believed that I would find love.
I believed before I turned twenty, I would find my special someone.
But I am not my mother.
And I'm nothing like my brother,
I didn't find the love of my life at sixteen.
I didn't live that teenage dream.
Instead, I wasted so much time,
Time and energy on a dream that wasn't mine.

But now I have found real love,
I have a love for life.
And so much love for my friends,
That is a different form of love,
It is a love that never ends.

Take Responsibility for Yourself

It's easy to blame,
It's easy to hate,
It's so easy to point out other people's mistakes,
You've made a list but left out your own name.

Start taking responsibility,
Stop acting like you didn't do anything.

Stop making excuses,
It's gone on for too long.
The time has come for you to admit,
That you are also the one that has done wrong.

For me

All this time I have been trying to be something more,
Wanting to understand who it was all for.
But now with brand new eyes I can finally see,
All these changes, all this time,
I have been doing it all for me.